FEARLESS

7 DAYS A WEEK

Michelle —
Many blessings to you
& your sweet family
for a fearless life!

Kim
Hamilton

KIM HAMILTON

ISBN 978-0-123456-789

Editor: Judy Beltis

Cover Design by Kim Daniels. (KimberlyDanielsPhotography.com)

Compass Provided by Elaina Louise Studios (ElainaLouiseStudios.com)

Format and Layout Design: Rob Moore (Mozaek.com)

This book is dedicated to my sweet family – Dave, Zack, Kelsey and Kaylee. I love you!

My deepest thanks to my dear friends who encouraged, helped, edited, and supported this journey!

Thank you especially to Judy Beltis for being the "Editor in Chief" who spent countless hours proofing and editing and sharing your wisdom, insight and encouragement!

Thank you to Kim Daniels (Kimberlydanielsphotography.com) for pouring in your photography and graphic skills to bring beauty to what fearless should look like.

Finally, thanks be to God for His indescribable gift of Jesus, for in Him is where I find life and breath and healing and direction!

Foreword

Kim Hamilton is a gifted musician and skilled communicator. Her music comes from the depths of her soul and her story has been developed in the crucible of living life. From the low points of deep sorrow to haunting fear, Kim developed her strength in the Lord especially as it was expressed through music, pouring from her heart in worship. Her journey is one of encouragement, of power and of hope. She tells her stories with convincing clarity and conviction.

You will not want to miss any part of the story or insight from God's Word that this woman of faith brings in "FEARLESS".

Graydon Jessup
Pastor, Boulder Valley Christian Church,
The Jonathon Project
Heart and Soul90

Introduction

I've heard it said that it takes 21 days repeating something to make a habit stick. To live beyond and above fear may be a lifelong goal that needs nurturing every day of life, way past 21 days. In my life's journey, I have found circumstances pop up around every turn that can produce fear or faith in my heart. God wants so much more for us than living a life dominated by fear. His strength gives us the ability to rise above and see beyond each trial. His desire is for us to use each difficulty to develop our character and speak of His greatness. I have heard and read that for years, but did not "know" God's unsurpassing peace and strength until the last few years. He is so faithful.

This 30 day devotional is full of scriptures that have strengthened my heart in difficult moments. God's Word is always fresh, true and unwavering. I hope you are encouraged and gain faith as you delve into His strength and let go of your weakness.

Many blessings,

Kim

Day One

"Are not two sparrows sold for a copper coin? Yet not one of them falls to the ground apart from your Father's will. So don't be afraid. You are worth much more than sparrows."

Matt. 10: 29,31

He is there. Isn't that an amazing verse? It makes you want to stop, take a deep breath, and ponder the capacity of our great and powerful God to carry the concerns of all creation in His heart. If the God of the Universe troubles Himself over what happens to tiny birds in midflight, think how much greater is His attentiveness to what happens to you and me. As Jesus Himself said, we are worth much more than sparrows. What an insight Jesus gives us into the heart of His Father!

Think about all the things God takes care of every day just to sustain life on this planet, making sure temperature, gravity, and the speed of the earth's rotation are at just the right settings. Think of how much attention it must take to oversee the great oceans and all the teeming life within them. And how would you like to have the responsibility of keeping all plant and animal life alive and reproducing and bearing fruit? Or of keeping the sky up where it should be?

All of this and more is incessantly on our Creator's mind. And yet...*you have not slipped from His notice.* He is not too busy to be involved in your daily life, nor is He too preoccupied with things more important than your well-being. It is He who keeps your individual heart beating, your own lungs breathing, and your every need under His watchfulness and care. And beyond all of this, amidst the great busyness of being the God of the Universe and in charge of everything, *He hears you* each and every time you call out to Him. In the most frightening of moments, Always. Every time. He may run the whole world, but He runs to your aid as well.

What if you woke up every morning with this understanding of God's heart toward you? Wouldn't you find yourself running in His direction?

Dear Almighty God,

Thank You for being such a huge, amazing God and yet a tenderly loving Father at the same time! Thank You for the steadfast care You provide for Your children. Help me today to let go of each fear as it comes and to rest instead in Your great strong hands that will guide me through this day.

_____

_____

_____

_____

_____

_____

Day Two

"She is clothed with strength and dignity, and she laughs with no fear of the future."

Prov. 31:25

What do you see when you read this verse? Do you see yourself? If I am honest, I have to admit that I don't see me. But what I do picture is an older saint - a classy lady with silver hair who's made it through the hard stuff with great style. You know the one. When she walks into the room people don't literally bow but they take notice and admire her for her strength and wisdom. Her beauty runs so deep one cannot miss it.

To be a woman with that type of character seems unattainable. In our own strength, it is. But when we remember that God is the one who clothes us with strength and dignity and that He is the source of that strength – it can change our perception of ourselves. We *are* strong. Ha! Even the world tells us that! Women are strong! Oh yeah! But inside, where we are weak, only God gives us the strength and beautiful dignity to live without fear.

Thank God for His mercy in helping you become that picture every new day.

Gracious Father,

Thank you for the strength and beauty You pour over me today. I give you my doubts, my fears, and my many faults. And I ask You to use me today as you wish. Amen.

_____

_____

_____

_____

_____

_____

Day Three

"Do not be afraid for I am with you. Do not be dismayed for I am your God. I will strengthen you, I will help you, I will uphold you with my victorious right hand."

Isaiah 41:10

Oh, how thankful I am for this verse! The Lord has inscribed it on my heart. It speaks to me of the depth of His love for us and of the compassion He has toward His frail children. In it I see proof of His knowledge of our need to hear repeatedly the affirmation that He is right there beside us and we need not be afraid, no matter what we are walking through.

A dear friend sent me a card with this verse on it just a few days before I was to undergo a bi-lateral mastectomy in 2008. It went with me, handwritten on an index card, on surgery day. It stayed in my hand through two hours of lymphatic mapping, a barrage of pre-operative prep procedures, and an anxious period of waiting until my doctor appeared and said it was time to go into the operating room. It also accompanied me there, although I wasn't allowed to hold it during my surgery. But when I awoke in recovery, the nurse attending me put the index card back in my hand and said, "Here is your verse. We all read it and prayed for you." The Lord had seen to it that His Word was spoken over me throughout the entire ordeal and I was remarkably free from fear. He did what He said He would do.

God's Word is not only absolutely victorious but it is strengthening beyond all reason. I guess it brings that peace which passes understanding.

I do not have this fear thing mastered yet. But each day as I say and sing this verse and plant it in the deepest recesses of my heart, I am learning to trust the God who is always with me and whose truth can conquer my every fear.

Gracious Father,

Thank you for your amazing, powerful Word! As I release my fears today, I thank you that You will strengthen, help, and uphold me through every moment. Thank You for the work You will do today in my life.

_____

_____

_____

_____

_____

_____

Day Four

"The athlete who trains, the musician who practices, the researcher who studies – each works toward a goal and must endure great testing."

Anonymous

We live in a society that admires professional and successful athletes, actors, and musicians. We are all attracted to qualities visible to the eye as we observe these prominent people - things like physical strength, or the ability to make a comeback after a failure, or just good old-fashioned achievement. What we tend to overlook, however, is the long, hard road of focused effort that each of these individuals had to follow in order to reach that place of excellence. What we fail to recognize is one of the primary characteristics required for a successful life - an overcoming spirit.

You will seldom hear a success story that does not tell of great personal sacrifice: hours spent in practice, discipline, and training; years devoted to gleaning from coaches, teachers, and mentors; and relentless honing of skills over a prolonged period of time. Aside from all of that, most of our heroes could also speak of moments of great suffering and personal loss and circumstances of extreme adversity. If we asked them if they ever felt like quitting or were afraid of the future, or did they go through great trials to get where they are, their answer would be a resounding "YES!" It's just the way life is, both for the great and the small. The difference between the two is the determination to push through what frightens us or seems too hard to face.

Rick Warren says in his book *The Purpose Driven Life*, "God is not concerned with our comfort nearly as much as our character." What a precise statement of God's purpose in allowing life's challenges to come between us and our goals! He is bound and determined to make overcomers of us and by what better means could He do it than to give us things that need to be overcome! Let's make His goal our own so that when - not *if* - difficulties come, we can embrace rather than fear them, and accept them for the character-refining instruments they are.

Father God,

Thank You ahead of time for whatever this day holds for me. Give me eyes to see the long-term picture of what You have in mind when You allow obstacles to come, and the faith to trust You when I don't understand what's happening. Please don't let me miss a minute of practicing, ministering, and loving in Your name due to fear or lack of perseverance. Make me an over-comer!

_____

_____

_____

_____

_____

_____

Day Five

"He will shield you with his wings. He will shelter you with his feathers. His faithful promises are your armor and protection."

Psalm 91:4

Each year when springtime comes, a pair of birds build a nest in the rafters near our front door. Our family daily watches the process of the birds preparing the nest and then when the babies come, we delight in hearing the little bitty chirps that come from it. The mama bird faithfully sits on the eggs and then remains to watch closely over her babies once they hatch. The daddy bird is never far away and is always at his protective post. If we walk too closely to his little family, he is sure to let us know we are trespassing by flying right at us in high-speed warning. (I must admit we are somewhat of a torment to the bird family because we get a ladder and climb right up close so we can see what's going on in the nest.) What an amazing and fascinating thing to see how much hard work and sacrifice these two parents pour out to protect and care for their own. How beautiful the knowledge that the God of the Universe and the Lord of our hearts does all that, and even more, for us!

I recently saw a cartoon posted on Facebook. In it, a man asks God to protect him. In the next frame he gets hit in the head with a rock! Understandably, he feels compelled to cry out, "Why, God? Why?" In the last picture, you see Jesus with both arms spread out blocking an avalanche of rocks that had been headed straight towards the man. "Sorry," Jesus says. "I missed one. Are you alright?"

God never tires, never waivers, never leaves, and is always looking out for our good. Remember – there is safety ever available to us if we will seek shelter under His wings. There is guaranteed protection for us against fear and worry if we will armor our souls with the promises He has so graciously provided in His Word.

Lord God,

Thank you for your gentle, loving, never-ending care. May I learn to stop and stay under Your wing of protection and guidance.

_____

_____

_____

_____

_____

_____

Day Six

"There is no room in love for fear. Well-formed love banishes fear. Since fear is crippling, a fearful life - fear of death, fear of judgment - is one not yet fully formed in love."

I John 4:18

What does God's love look like? The Bible tells us He loves us with an *agape* love. This is a Greek word for the unconditional, sacrificial love that can only come from God Himself. It is a quality found only in the Divine. Human beings fall far short in their efforts to love God - or each other - like God loves us. I would argue that part of the reason for that is our fear.

When we love someone, we have expectations of that love being returned to us. If we have reason to doubt this, or have suffered disappointment in the past, we pull back in fear and temper our love with wariness or withdraw it altogether. If we have the slightest suspicion that the love we give someone else is not reciprocated in equal measure, we live in fear of abandonment. And when abandonment happens we live in fear of the uncertain future. This cycle lessens our capacity to give or receive unconditional love, or even understand what it really is. Is it any wonder that God's Word speaks so clearly about the effects of fear on the quality of our love?

I am mindful of divorce in our society and how it has redefined our concept of what love is supposed to do and be. The love upon which many marriages are formed today doesn't look much like God's kind of love at all. God just loves. He gives us free will and when we walk away, He still loves. He watches and waits for our return, feeling the pain of our rejection (yes, God *feels*) and He still loves. When we finally make our way back to Him, He forgives unreservedly. Still God loves. God has no fear in Him to taint His love for us. God just loves.

Sadly, I am one of the many who have walked through divorce, and that after I had done everything in my power to save my marriage. I continued to love and serve God as I always had. I worked hard to forgive my husband's faults and admitted to my own. When it all fell apart, I turned to Christ for the healing and joy I desperately needed. I did everything I could possibly think of to do to recover from the grief and the loss. But as much as I did all of that, I've still had to face the truth of the matter: the journey through divorce planted fear in my heart at the thought of loving again.

As I continue to think through these things each day I am resolved to overcome the fear that would keep me from loving as I want to - as God wants me to. He is teaching me that real love does not worry about what is given in return or what may fail in the future. It is concerned only with blessing those precious others He has put us in relationship with in the here and now, fully living and fully giving each other fear-free love.

Loving Father,

Thank You for Your amazing example of love. May I love more freely and fully.

_____

_____

_____

_____

_____

_____

Day Seven

"There the angel of the Lord appeared to him in flames of fire from within a bush. Moses saw that though the bush was on fire it did not burn up. So Moses thought, 'I will go over and see this strange sight—why the bush does not burn up.' When the Lord saw that he had gone over to look, God called to him from within the bush, 'Moses! Moses!' And Moses said, 'Here I am.' 'Do not come any closer,' God said. 'Take off your sandals, for the place where you are standing is holy ground.' Then he said, 'I am the God of your father, the God of Abraham, the God of Isaac and the God of Jacob.' At this, Moses hid his face, because he was afraid to look at God."

Exodus 3:3-6

Imagine this. You're driving along to the mall and, Voila! A burning bush right in front of you! Not only is it burning, it's not even being consumed by the fire! Such a sight would certainly get our attention. The same was true for Moses.

When Moses saw this astonishing thing he went over to check it out up close and personal. Little did he know that he was walking into the most life-changing encounter he would ever have. Moses stumbled upon the Lord's Presence.

The circumstances may be different, but God still works like that with us today. His Presence can take us unawares at any moment, in any place of His choosing. It can be frightening. It can be comforting. It can be quiet and reverent. It can be joyous and exhilarating. But however He gets us there, whether we stand in awe, delight, or abject fear before Him, we are shaken out of the ordinariness of our lives into something quite "extra-ordinary." And we know it is a moment when we cannot fail to give Him our complete attention.

"Take off your sandals, Moses, you are standing on holy ground," said the Lord. "Uh, ok. Absolutely. Done!" Wouldn't we respond in the same way? "Whatever You say, Lord! Right away!" An overwhelming sense of awe and reverence ushers us into the place of perfect obedience. It's so much easier to follow directions when you get them firsthand from Someone who holds your life in His hands, Someone you love and respect and would do anything to please.

Moses was am*bush*ed (pun intended) by the Lord's Presence that day on the mountainside. Sometimes that's the way it happens with us, too, but it doesn't have to be like that. The Word tells us that we can take the initiative – *we* can seek *Him* and He will be found by us! We have access to His Presence at the throne of grace anytime we have need. The only condition is that we want this with all our heart. I pray that daily each of us will want this experience with Him. I pray that we will seek Him, find Him, fall before Him in awestruck worship, listen carefully to what He would tell us to do, and then go do it! Instead of a burning bush, Lord, give us burning hearts for You.

Father, I live today with thanks and in awe of who You are.

_____

_____

_____

_____

_____

_____

Day Eight

Fearless: assured,   bold,   courageous,   gutsy,   heroic,   sassy, undaunted, and wise.

What definition do you think of when you hear the word "fearless?"   Is it how you characterize children in their innocent adventures, before they become "old enough to know better?"   Do you see it as a reckless, irresponsible attitude that some people never grow out of?   Is fearlessness even attainable once we reach adulthood, having acquired so much knowledge of good and evil along the way? Is living fearlessly only for some?

We can easily picture certain other people who have the "right stuff" to pull it off.   The first men on the moon were "heroic." Firefighters are "courageous."   Dr. Martin Luther King, Jr. was "bold." It's really not hard to think of others who just seem to have been born with the qualities needed to live fearlessly.   But what about the rest of us?

The Scriptures would indicate that I am called to live a courageous life.   Me?   I'm just an ordinary person!   And I have circumstances that bring fear to my heart every waking day.   Yet the single most oft-repeated command in the Word is this one: "Do not be afraid!"   Since God does not ask us to do anything He will not empower us for, what exactly is expected of me here?   Where do I find a boldness that is not naturally within me but God clearly wants me to have?

The answer lies in seeing myself the way God sees me.   When I comprehend how deeply He loves me and how faithfully He is present in my every circumstance, I discover a new level of boldness in everything I do.   Boldness that is rooted in God's unchanging love for me changes everything else!   I can love more deeply.   I can give more freely.   I can serve more wholeheartedly.   I can live – really live – and not miss out on a single thing that fear would otherwise deprive me of.   It turns out that the "right stuff" for fearless living is available to even the most timid of souls. Fearlessness is simply trusting God.

"Do not worry about your life, what you will eat or drink; or about your body, what you will wear. Is not life more important than food, and the body more important than clothes? Who of you by worrying can add a single hour to his life?"

Matthew 6:25,27

Merciful Savior,

Give me strength to live with courage, boldness, and wisdom. I long to live the life You have created for me.

_____

_____

_____

_____

_____

_____

Day Nine

"For I am the Lord your God who takes hold of your right hand and says to you, Do not fear; I will help you."

Isaiah 41:13

Have you have ever gone rock climbing and repelling? I recall that experience vividly from my high school and college days. I especially remember the crystal clear, cool mornings when we would begin the climb up the backside of the mountain, hiking up hills and crevices, walking through creeks, and helping each other along. This part of the day was great fun and loud with laughter, chatter, and singing. But once we reached the top and looked out over the sights before us something would happen. Silence. Wow! The beauty was breathtaking. And so was the sheerness of the cliff face plummeting below us – the one we would be expected to step off of.

I remember gladly letting others go first and watched as our guides harnessed these excited people up. That's not exactly how it felt for me. In all honesty, I wanted to make sure they survived before I gave it a try. When my turn came, my knees were shaking so badly I was sure I would fall to my death just trying to get into the harness. I was thinking, "That little thing is all that's going to hold me? Really? That man tying off the rope and holding my life in his hands - does he know how much I want to get home safely? My youth pastor says this will be good for me and my faith life. Is he crazy?"

The nice guide man instructed each person to step to the edge of the cliff, face backwards, and stand out with only our toes touching terra firma. What? His next words were, "When you are ready, just step backwards." You've got to be kidding, right? But finally, with a deep breath of determination, and strength from some hidden reserve of faith, I stepped out into thin air.

There's no describing a moment like that. The sense of pushing beyond a barrier that both fear and reason tell you not to cross and then actually surviving the thing is both terrifying and exhilarating. I have experienced that exact same feeling at certain key events of my life: driving a car for the first time, going off to college, walking down the aisle to get married, or giving birth to a baby. These were breathtaking moments I eagerly stepped into, with full expectation of safely reaching solid ground. But what happens when life forces us over the cliff without our consent?

Darker seasons can plunge us into pain and change we didn't ask for. These are times that also take our breath away but in a manner that feels more like having the wind knocked out of us. Yet even then we can end up landing safely, though it may be in a place not of our choosing. For these are the moments when we are given opportunity to come to really know that we wouldn't have come out alive at all but for Jesus' catching us. Jesus, the Author and Perfector of our faith, spurs us on to ever-greater leaps of faith and is our safety net at all times.

When you glance at the cover of this book wherever it may lie, take notice of the shoes and the compass. These feminine, yet sturdy shoes that sit ready to take a step out in faith over fear represent each one of us. The compass is the key. Consistently keeping the focus to the true north, and trusting God to direct each path changes every journey. I pray that this is a visual that resonates with you, reminding you that you never walk alone. Your Savior gives you strength and security and courage. And right alongside is a whole army of women just like you.

Powerful God,

Thank You for extending Your right hand to me and for just leaving it there waiting for me to grab hold of when I need it. Your patience and trust in me amazes me. Thank You for the previous steps of faith that have shown me who You are, and thank You, Lord, that for the rest of my days, any step of faith I take will lead me directly to You and further into Your eternal, rich, deep plan for my life.

_____

_____

_____

_____

_____

_____

Day Ten

"Even though Jesus was God's Son, he learned obedience from the things he suffered."

Hebrews 5:8

Are you sitting down? This could be one of those "aha" moments. Just soak this in a little bit. *Jesus learned obedience through suffering.* Who would have guessed that the Creator of the whole universe would have to learn anything! Or that the Son of God Himself would have to be taught obedience! Isn't that a mind-blowing concept? Well, here's another one. If we are to be like Jesus, our learning path will be the same as His; our character formation will come at great personal cost and it won't be easy. In fact, I'm sure that part of what Jesus was doing here was showing us how it's done.

Jesus went through loneliness, temptation, and stress. He never had a nice house to live in, and sometimes no home at all. He worked at a very physical job in carpentry, and walked the countryside for years as an itinerant preacher. He was subjected to criticism, ridicule, rejection, physical pain, separation from family, meager finances, and personal betrayal. And that's only a partial listing of what He tasted living here on earth in the form of a human being. If God required His one and only Son to go through all those things so that He could work His perfect plan through Jesus' life, why would He exempt us from the same? The Bible says that even Jesus, who was God in the flesh, "was made perfect through suffering." I would say we are in very good company when it comes to suffering through life's difficulties.

What might God be up to when He allows tough things to come our way? Maybe that's the question we should be asking instead of "why is this happening to me?" None of us want to undergo the painful rigors of character developing trials — I am with you on that one! But Romans 5 says "suffering produces perseverance; perseverance, character; and character, hope." Oh, how I long for that character and hope; I would just prefer it without the suffering.

Take comfort in this thought: If the pain is great, the purpose is greater. We can't always see what God is accomplishing through the circumstances that try us, but we can be certain that something mighty in His Kingdom is being done. Isn't that exactly what Jesus' life and death proved? Let us be worthy of the title we usually relegate to Him alone. Follow Him in His role as suffering servant.

Jesus,

I stand in awe that you would come to live as an example for me through suffering!

_____

_____

_____

_____

_____

_____

Day Eleven

"That night the Lord said to Gideon, 'Get up! Go down into the Midianite camp, for I have given you victory over them! But if you are afraid to attack, go down to the camp with your servant Purah. Listen to what the Midianites are saying, and you will be greatly encouraged. Then you will be eager to attack.' So Gideon took Purah and went down to the edge of the enemy camp."

Judges 7:9-11

God and Gideon had been having an ongoing conversation. It all started when the Lord showed up one day as Gideon was threshing wheat and told him that he was about to become his people's next great military hero. At the time, Israel was under terrible oppression from their foes, the Midianites, and to say that Gideon received his marching orders with doubt and reluctance is putting it mildly. Gideon clearly thought this was a case of mistaken identity.

You gotta love Gideon for his transparency with God. "If this is really You," he says, "and I'm not imagining things, make the dew collect on this fleece I'm going to lay out, but let the ground all around it remain dry." When the Lord did exactly that, Gideon pushed further. "Okay, just so I can be absolutely certain that it's You, let's do it the other way around." Sure enough, the Lord provided the requested proof.

But God wanted to make Gideon surer than that. "You have too big an army to go up against these tens of thousands of Midianites," He told him. "How about we whittle your forces down to say, 300, and that way when you win you'll know beyond a shadow of a doubt that it was Me. And if you're still afraid to go, sneak down to the Midianite camp and eavesdrop on their conversations; when you hear how I plan to deliver them into your hand, it'll make you feel better." Gideon did just that. Perhaps by this time he was hoping that God would fail the test so that he could just go home and get back to winnowing grain. But once again the Lord's words proved reassuringly true and Gideon found he had the courage to keep going on this crazy mission. Then the mission got crazier.

"Here's the battle plan," said the Lord. "All 300 of you get a horn, a jar, and a torch. When Gideon gives the signal, blow your horns and break your jars and raise your torches. That's how the victory will be won."

Kind of sounds like David going up against Goliath with a slingshot and a couple of stones, doesn't it? Kind of sounds ridiculous and impossible...until you understand that on the ancient battlefield, torches and horns were carried by the leaders of companies of 100 men each, and the sight of 300 approaching torches would make the Midianites believe 30,000 Israelites were coming their way...until you understand the unnerving effect that 300 battle horns blaring forth in the darkness would have on an unsuspecting and taken-by-surprise enemy...until you understand that the breaking of the jars was intended to emulate the sound of thousands of swords being drawn from their scabbards in preparation for attack...all of which threw the Midianites into panic and led to their defeat.

I love that we are allowed to watch how Gideon processes all this. I love even more that we get to see how God worked him through fear and disbelief at each point in his journey into destiny. You see, God knew exactly what He was doing all along, but what's most endearing to me is that He compassionately took into account the fact that Gideon did not.

So it is with you and I. We all feel like cowards at one time or another, fearing to do things that the Lord has asked of us – especially when His methodology collides with our reason. Remember Gideon and be reminded that the God who knows what things you fear looks upon you with patience and affection as you struggle to put feet to your obedience. He will show you things along the way that make the needed leaps of faith possible. Like Gideon, you will hear the words, *"The Lord is with you, you mighty [woman] of valor."*

Lord God,

Thank You that Your ways and wisdom are much higher and wiser, and very much different from ours. I praise You for Your patience with Gideon, and with me. I am so grateful that You use the smallest steps of trust and obedience to grow us into giants of faith. I pray that today I will trust you enough to lay out fleeces with no fear of condemnation, and to follow Your instructions with no fear of things turning out badly. Amen.

_____

_____

_____

_____

_____

_____

Day Twelve

"The ultimate measure of a man is not where he stands in moments of comfort and convenience but where he stands at moments of challenge and controversy."

Martin Luther King Jr.

Dr. King said it well in that quote. He's not really saying anything we don't know, but the wisdom in his statement grabs us.

How often have we expressed indignation and disappointment when high-profile, popular celebrities or politicians fall into ruin as a result of sordid personal scandals? If our esteem for people is built on nothing more than a shallow public persona, why are we surprised when their moral failures reveal their true colors? And why is our society so mesmerized by such public figures in the first place?

Beauty, wealth, and popularity do not make the person. Rather it is the moral compass one looks to in moments of temptation to take the easy way out or turn a blind eye to what is inconvenient to see. That is where character is both revealed and formed. These are moments that mold and change us and cause us to bring blessings or heartache to others.

Perhaps we should keep our admiration in check long enough to observe how someone walks through adversity and then decide what we think is true about them. And if integrity shines through, be thankful for that admirable person and to the One who provides them the strength to stand.

"Greater is He that is in you than he that is in the world." I John 4:4

Great Sovereign God,

Thank you for Your presence in every moment of my life. Father, grant me Your strength and wisdom to be able to stand tall and confidently walking through each day, knowing You are in control. Thank You for entrusting me with the challenges You know I can handle with Your strength, knowing all the while they will shape and mold me as I follow You faithfully.

_____

_____

_____

_____

_____

_____

Day Thirteen

"I lie down and sleep; I wake again, because the Lord sustains me. I will not fear the tens of thousands drawn up against me on every side."

Psalm 3:5,6

There is a song written and recorded by Nichole Nordeman called "Small Enough" which has repeatedly ministered to my heart throughout the last several years. I first heard it when I was walking through my battle with breast cancer. I was captured by the lyrics because they gave me an entirely fresh and new concept of the God I thought I already knew so well. It was a revelation that came just when I needed it and it spoke to me exactly what I needed to hear.

I had always seen God as great and big and magnificent. Majestic. All-Powerful. The Mighty God who created the universe and designed the heavens and is the Savior of all mankind! Everything I pictured about Him was, in a word, BIG! And He is, in fact, all that and more, so I was right to regard Him with reverent awe. But the problem was that "big" carried with it the connotation of being "distant," and in the middle of many a troubled night worrying about all that was happening to me, I needed a God I could feel close to. That's why I think He made sure I heard these words from Nordeman's song:

"...and I know you could leave writing
on the wall that's just for me
or send wisdom while I'm sleeping,
like in Solomon's sweet dreams
but I don't need the strength of Samson
or a chariot in the end
just want to know that you still know
how many hairs are on my head
oh great God, be small enough to hear me now"

Copyright 2000 Ariose Music. Used by permission.

I had never thought about a God who could make Himself small enough to hear the faintest whisper on my lips. And the concept of Him taking the trouble to count the hairs on your head takes on a world of new meaning for someone undergoing chemotherapy. Can you imagine the comfort I felt when the great and mighty God of the whole universe revealed Himself like that to me? How much more tender and personal could He be? How thankful I am for this new understanding of Him.

Sisters, be assured of this: when the situation calls for it, He absolutely will be small enough for you to detect Him right there beside you! No matter what you face, no matter what enemies come against you, your Great God hears and sees and heals.

Oh Great God,

Thank you Lord that you hear our faintest whisper. Thank you for your inspired Word that brings clarity and strength. For all that You have done, we say thanks.

_____

_____

_____

_____

_____

_____

Day Fourteen

"If the Son has set you free, then you are free indeed."

John 8:36

Free? Free? Really? Most of us women love a good sale, right? "Buy one, get one free" often sets us off on a shopping spree. Any "free gift to the first 200 customers" is sure to entice us through the door of a store we're passing by. And how fun is it to call into a radio station to win free concert tickets? Or, better yet, to sit through a delightful vacation ownership presentation to "win" a free week of vacation somewhere? Do those all sound familiar?

The word "free" is thrown around pretty loosely these days but many of the offers and promises held out to us actually come with strings attached. Yet we continue to be drawn in by the attractive prospect of getting something for nothing. So how do we respond to Jesus' statement that He has a particular brand of freedom for us, which is in itself a free offer – a free offer of freedom, so to speak? What is this freedom that Christ says is ours for the taking, and is it really free of charge?

When Jesus talks about setting us free He means it in the sense of being released from the obligations and penalties of a system of law (in this case, the Old Testament Mosaic law which had been in effect in Israel for about 1400 years). This law was given by God as a means of "settling accounts" between Himself and sinful man, but it was a heavy burden on the people, requiring them to live by a strict code of religious rituals and blood atonement through animal sacrifices. It was like living under a never-ending checklist of things that must be done to gain the Lord's favor, coupled with unrelenting guilt for sin. There was a high price to be paid for peace with God, and up until the time of Jesus, keeping the Mosaic law was the only way to purchase it.

Jesus changed everything. By His sacrifice on the cross He met every legal requirement of the law. He paid the price for every sin you and I would ever commit. He shed His blood for the forgiveness of our sins and He set us free from any guilt associated with them. Once mankind was a slave under the yoke of the law of sin and death but that is no longer the case – we are free of all that now if we accept what Jesus did on our behalf. The word "indeed" adds weight to the quality of that freedom: it means "truly, absolutely, in reality, and as a point of fact. "If the Son has set you free, you ARE free indeed!"

Here lies the ultimate offer you can't refuse. The God who created beautiful sunsets and rainbows, who created squirrels and fall leaves and every other thing in the world that delights you; the God who formed you and loves you - it is this same God who sets you free! You are set free from your sins and any resulting guilt or heartache that tries to cling to you. Knowing God and finding these truths in His Word will bring you to a fresh, real, continual place of freedom!

Gracious Lord, thank you for unmerited freedom!

_____

_____

_____

_____

_____

_____

Day Fifteen

"The next time you find yourself alone in a dark alley facing the undeniables of life, don't cover them with a blanket, or ignore them with a nervous grin. Don't turn up the TV and pretend they aren't there. Instead, stand still, whisper His name, and listen. He is nearer than you think."

Max Lucado (Upwords)

One of my very favorite authors is Max Lucado. He has such a God-given gift for expressing the truths of Scripture in an understandable way. He makes it so easy to see the spiritual side of things in the daily grind. Can you find yourself in this quote from his book *Upwords*? Does the nervous grin sound familiar? Or the easy escape into the alternate reality of media or technology? How ironic is it that some of the most popular TV shows these days are reality shows. Other people's realities have become a form of entertainment. Any reality will do, it seems, as long as it isn't our own. At all costs, we must be able to escape that! But sometimes we can't.

A good friend of mine who was on a missions trip to Haiti back in January of 2010, found herself alone on a rooftop when the city of Port-au-Prince was struck by a devastating, destructive earthquake. She had been serving at an orphanage sponsored by our church, and after a busy day, had slipped away for a few quiet minutes with the Lord before dinnertime. I remember her telling us how she watched house after house falling to the ground as the realization of what was taking place hit her. Recognizing there was absolutely nowhere she could run to for safety she had no choice but to stay right there on the roof. All of a sudden she heard herself screaming into the sky at the top of her lungs, "Jesus! Jesus! Jesus!" The building she was standing on stayed up and did not fall. My friend had instinctively sought refuge in the strongest shelter there is – the name of Jesus.

Her experience is a testimony to one of the most important teachings of the New Testament: in the name of Jesus there is supernatural, unsurpassable, available power – power we have been given access to by Jesus' death, burial, and resurrection as King of

Kings and Lord of Lords; power we were meant to appropriate to carry out the King's business here on earth; power we can call on to help us stand against trouble, fear, and the devil himself.

The Bible tells us that the name of Jesus effects healing and deliverance. The lame walk and the blind see; the dead are resurrected and sinners rise up cleansed to walk in new life. His is the name above all names, and even the demons shudder at it. All spiritual power and authority are given those who call themselves by His name, and no power of the enemy can harm them. *"The name of the Lord is a strong tower;"* sings the psalmist, *"the righteous run into it and they are safe."* We of the New Covenant know this name to be Jesus, and as my friend in Haiti discovered, there is no safer place we can be.

The next time you're cornered in the dark alley, speak His name into your situation. Release the power and peace that reside in it. You don't have to shout it from the rooftop; a fear-filled whisper will suffice. The power comes not from the strength of your voice, but from the strength of the name of Jesus.

"...He gave him a name that is above every other name, so that at the name of Jesus every knee will bow, in heaven and on earth and under the earth"

Philippians 2:9,10

Jesus, Jesus, Jesus!

As the old chorus says, there's just something about that name. You are the rock that we build our life upon. You are our hope for the future. We speak Your name today, Jesus, knowing You are faithful , true, and all-powerful. Thank You for releasing Your power into our lives through Your beautiful, wonderful name.

_____

_____

_____

_____

_____

_____

Day Sixteen

"The LORD had said to Abram, 'Leave your native country, your relatives, and your father's family, and go to the land that I will show you. I will make you into a great nation. I will bless you and make you famous, and you will be a blessing to others. I will bless those who bless you and curse those who treat you with contempt. All the families on earth will be blessed through you.' So Abram departed as the LORD had instructed, and Lot went with him. Abram was seventy-five years old when he left Haran."

Genesis 12:1-4

So here's the short version. At age 75, God told Abraham to leave his country, his family, and his lifelong home to go to an unknown location where God would lead him. The details of the journey would be given on a need to know basis. He was not told what to pack, who should go with him, or where he would find food along the way, all questions that had to be going through his mind.

I don't know about you, but I would be somewhat fearful in that situation. In our comfortable lives, just to move from one house to another is a big deal, and Lord forbid we should have to go as far as some other state! We worry, we plan, we pack, and we scour the area for the best neighborhoods to live in. In fact, it would be considered downright irresponsible of us if we didn't do all that work up front so that we know what we're getting into. We go to great lengths to learn everything we possibly can about what lies ahead. Even so, the ordeal of moving has been identified as one of the highest stress-inducing experiences in modern day life.

What kind of faith did this man Abraham have, that he was able to pack it all up, not even knowing where he was going, and hit the wide-open road just because the Lord told him to do it? He was not exactly in the prime of his life. In fact, I'm sure he never expected that, having reached the age of 75, he'd be asked to go somewhere else and start all over again. And can you imagine the conversation between he and his wife Sarah when he told her what they were going to do?

The faith that Abraham had in God was outlandish and outstanding. And that's the point of his story. A man who could believe God like that would have a very unique relationship with Him, and would be shown even greater wonders: like a firstborn son at the age of 100 years and like a promise that his descendants would be as numerous as the stars and inherit a land flowing with milk and honey, and like a sneak preview glimpse of God's gospel plan to save the world through a sacrificial Lamb.

Abraham's faith earned him favor with God. The same can be true for us. We also may be led down unpredictable roads, and there's no guarantee that the way will be easy – even if it's the one chosen for us by the Lord. But if we follow Abraham's example, trustingly walking by faith and not by sight, He promises us amazing things to come.

Lord God,

Give me courage like Abraham to say, "Where You go, I'll go; where You lead, I'll follow." Amen.

_____

_____

_____

_____

_____

Day Seventeen

"Life isn't about waiting for the storm to pass, it's about learning to dance in the rain."

Unknown Author

Our ten-year-old Lhasa Apso, Chrissy, does not like to go outside in any weather other than perfect sunshine. If it is windy, rainy, or just a little too cold, she will simply stand at the door and refuse to go out. If made to journey outside, she will then stay close to the door, visibly shaking, and present us with an altogether pitiful sight to behold. We have all taken our turns venturing out into the rain, walking and dancing and coaxing, in an effort to show her that she, too, will survive. (How I wish I had captured some of those Kodak moments!) Still, she does not believe it.

How much of that little Lhasa Apso dog lives in us? In the course of our lives we live through many storms, we get wet, we dry off, and we come out no worse for the wear. But do we live like we know that? Or do we shrink back from every little cloudburst, fearful of some discomfort we might have to suffer, and refusing to believe that we actually will survive this one too.

What if, when faced with the inevitable storms of life, we focused on God's sovereignty and His faithfulness in bringing us through the many storms past? The Bible instructs us to rejoice through trials, thanking God for them and finding joy at each turn. If we would take the time to look back at the ones we've already lived through, and call to mind how God got us through each and every one, we would probably decide that God is worthy of our trust after all. It's okay. We can follow Him out into the rain and even enjoy splashing in the puddles.

"We know that in all things God works for the good of those who love Him."

Romans 8:28

Oh Great God,

For the storms that have past and left us safe in Your arms, we thank You. For the weather ahead, we ask for Your joy and strength as we trust in Your goodness.

_____

_____

_____

_____

_____

_____

Day Eighteen

"Even though I walk through the valley of the shadow of death, I will fear no evil, for You are with me; Your rod and Your staff, they comfort me."

Psalm 23:4

This verse has brought comfort to countless families as they gather for a memorial service for a loved one. In that setting, it is often interpreted as meaning that we merely walk "through" the valley and do not stay there. It is a path leading straight into the arms of Almighty God. And that's a great comfort.

But what about the daily journeys we take in life? This verse is relevant there as well. No matter what valley or shadow or time of darkness we may walk through in the course of our lives, God tells us not to fear. He gives us the certain assurance that even then He is with us! God is with us!

If you are one who enjoys a good suspense movie, you recognize the components that create a sense of journeying through a scary situation. The lighting darkens to accentuate shadow and mystery, the music swells and builds the suspense, and the character deals with the antagonist in the story. We watch on pins and needles waiting to see how it's all going to turn out.

In the story of our lives, we know how it ends. God is victorious and He holds us in the palm of His hand. No matter how frightening the valley, we are coming out the other side intact! Being equipped with that truth helps us to walk less fearfully. We don't have to hide our eyes or feel the adrenaline rush in our gut. God is with us! That is the simple, blessed truth!

Father God,

As I walk through the valleys and hilltops of this day, help me to see the scenery, to really see You in all that I do. Your hand is powerful, Your rod and Your staff a strong protection.

Day Nineteen

"I am leaving you with a gift – peace of mind and heart. And the peace I give is a gift the world cannot give. So don't be troubled or afraid."

John 14:27

I have given my family many gifts over the years, as I'm sure you have. Some were expensive, some were less costly; some were thoughtful, others were just necessities disguised as "presents". (For years Santa put new battery-operated toothbrushes and socks in our kids' stockings). And some gifts missed the mark altogether. But you know, that's never the case with our gracious God. He knows exactly what we need and when we need it. He is acutely aware of what we are most lacking and He gives "a gift" to provide the perfect help for any situation. I just love that about Him, don't you?

In this day and age, the art of gift giving has reached an all-time peak of creativity and convenience. We have all given or received gift cards for manicures, massages, shopping, dining out, movies, free babysitting, and just about every other kind of merchandise or service under the sun. Gifts today are generous and extravagant and often express our desires to touch the heart or meet the need of another. But try as we might, we are not able to give a gift that supplies people what they really need. Even the gifts of relationship that we give each other do not quell the issues of the heart.

There is only One Gift-giver who can give the gifts that change lives. These gifts are peace, joy, strength, direction, courage, wisdom, love, patience, kindness – all given freely in limitless supply, all proceeding exclusively from Him. His gift of peace, for both mind and heart, far exceeds anything anyone in the world can give you. It is a gift designed with thought behind it for you! Open it and experience joy in it!

Giver of All Good Things,

You are so amazing! Father, thank You for the immeasurable, meaningful, powerful gifts You design for me. I claim Your gift of peace today!

Day Twenty

"Moses answered, 'What if they do not believe me or listen to me and say', 'The LORD did not appear to you?' Then the LORD said to him, 'What is that in your hand?' 'A staff,' he replied. The LORD said, 'Throw it on the ground.' Moses threw it on the ground and it became a snake, and he ran from it. Then the LORD said to him, 'Reach out your hand and take it by the tail.' So Moses reached out and took hold of the snake and it turned back into a staff in his hand. 'This,' said the LORD, 'is so that they may believe that the LORD, the God of their fathers—the God of Abraham, the God of Isaac and the God of Jacob—has appeared to you.'"

Exodus 4:1-5

I love how God's Father-Heart is demonstrated in this well-known passage of Scripture. He displays such tender loving-kindness towards us, His fearful children. Which one of us does not do on a regular basis what we see Moses do in this story? Our "what ifs" could probably fill a whole book were we to write them down, and we're not usually being asked to do anything even close to what was being asked of Moses.

It's almost comforting to see one of our great Bible heroes exhibiting the kind of fear and insecurity we often wrestle with. But what's more comforting than that is to see how God responds. Moses is not chastised, lectured, or told he just needs to have more faith. Moses' transparency with the Lord stirs up God's compassion, not His judgment. Gently, one step at a time, the Lord works Moses through his fear, reassuring him that he will not go alone to do the assigned task, nor will he be left hung out to dry when asked for proof of the Lord's hand in it. (It's interesting to me that in devising the sign that Moses was to take with him, the Lord chose something that Moses was obviously afraid of – a snake! Moses got an additional workout in pushing through his fears that day!)

What can we learn from all this? Is it that if we habitually live in the land of "what if," we don't have to hide it from God? (Not that we could do that anyway.) When we bring our "giants" openly before

Him, He will work with us. He will find a way for us and equip us to go there. He will guide us and reassure us through the thing *if* we will step out despite our fears and just do what He wants us to do. That's the essence of victorious living, finding confidence in Christ when there's none to be found in ourselves.

God has compassion on your fear. Live like you know that. Tell Him all about it and then go out and meet your challenges head-on!

Almighty God,

For this day, this very day, thank you for what will come. Help me to be faithful, bold, and humble. Thank you for the way you lead and guide me, especially when I am afraid.

_____

_____

_____

_____

_____

_____

Day Twenty-One

"You block your dream when you allow your fear to grow bigger than your faith."

Mary Manin Morrissey

My major in college was Music Ministry, with an emphasis in piano. Part of the requirement in obtaining my degree was to perform an hour-long senior recital mostly comprised of classical music that had to be memorized. Now, I was not a novice when it came to being in front of people and learning a lot of music. I had started playing the piano at church back when I was about ten years old, accompanying the choir during worship.

My job in college was to accompany vocal recitals for other students. I found that to be great fun. But when it came to a performance that rested squarely on my own shoulders, with no one else sharing the responsibility for the quality of the program, I started doubting that I was up to the challenge. I was scared to death of doing that recital.

My dream was to use music to bring people closer to the Lord. That's why I was at college studying music ministry in the first place. But as I faced the daunting task of learning songs, rehearsing vocalists, setting the stage design, and trying to invite enough family and friends to create a respectable audience, I began to fear the dream was going to slip out of my grasp. I just didn't believe I could pull it all off.

I was so worried about it that the week before the recital I had a car wreck. The day before, I got sick. If it were not for the encouragement of some very dear friends and professors I would have walked away from the whole thing. But I pulled myself together and showed up for the performance, even though my knees shook so badly during the first song that my foot wouldn't stay on the piano pedal!

Then as I began to relax into the music something amazing started to happen. I felt a new level of confidence and faith rise within me until I was absolutely certain I was playing by the strength of the Lord. He drew me to Himself and showed me what He could do through me when I didn't think I could do anything on my own. The whole event was a remarkable and unforgettable demonstration to me of God's provision.

Just think, if I had succumbed to my fears and not stood up to face what I was afraid of I never would have experienced Him the way I did that night. And I certainly would not have seen the fulfillment of my dream to minister in His name through music. As agonizing as it was, how thankful I am that He gave me that lesson in faith.

"If you have faith as small as a mustard seed, you can say to this mountain, 'Move from here to there,' and it will move. Nothing will be impossible for you."

Matthew 17:20

_____

_____

_____

_____

_____

_____

Day Twenty-Two

"The Lord is my light and my salvation. Whom shall I fear? The Lord is the stronghold of my life. Of whom shall I be afraid?"

Psalm 27:1

There is an old camp song based on this verse that we used to sing every year at summer camp. To give it an extra boost, and so that the kids would really remember it, we would sing it in the dark and have everyone turn on their flashlights when we got to the chorus. Then we'd all hold our lights up high over our heads and belt out the words as loud as we could: *"So I will not be afraid; no, I will not be afraid; for the Lord is my light and my salvation!"* It was just a simple, fun camp song, but it had the power to pierce the surrounding darkness with light and joyful sound. I think there's a simple but profound truth in that.

We live in a world that has a lot of darkness, both physically and spiritually speaking. Sometimes we feel like we're lost in it. Sometimes we've got to remind ourselves that there really is a Source of light out there that can never be overcome by it. Most of us are afraid of the dark to some degree, and we all have nights when we just have to have a flashlight nearby to dispel the darkness and ease our fears. (I believe that's what is known as "the dark night of the soul.") Well, here's the good news: Jesus is your Flashlight!

It was no chance remark Jesus was making when He called Himself the Light of the World. Not by a long shot. He knew exactly what would bring us comfort in our sorrows and courage in our weakness. He knew what would draw us to Him more than any other thing. People in darkness are always drawn to light, and like a moth to the flame, we are attracted to His.

He lights our way with His wisdom and guidance, and He illumines us in our confusion and ignorance. His light shines in our hearts and warms us with His love. His light brings us hope and peace, and we bask in the light of His grace. His light is a beacon of truth amidst deception; it's a place of safety in danger; it's the unapproachable place where He dwells and a means of displaying to us His transcendent glory. Jesus is all about the light – it's His very essence. Jesus IS the Light.

Jesus, the Light of the World, promises to always be with us. He goes before us, behind us, and alongside us. And His light goes with Him and illumines every step of our journey. This God who lights our way keeps us safe and accomplishes our salvation. He does that so that we will not be condemned to eternal darkness, but will live with Him in His Eternal Light. Carry the lamp of this Word in your heart and you, too, will pierce the darkness, singing at the top of your voice, "*I will not be afraid for the Lord is my Light!*"

My Great Stronghold,

I trust in You today. As I gain strength from You, I will be mindful to give you praise for the peace and direction at each turn. Thank you for being a loving, gentle shepherd!

Day Twenty-Three

"For God has not given us a spirit of fear, but of power, and of love, and of a sound mind."

II Timothy 1:7

Like you, I have probably read this verse many, many times; in fact, it's one of those verses many of us commit to memory. That's because it's such a powerful declaration of the truth that we don't have to live under the tyranny of a spirit of fear. That is never God's intention for us and we like hearing that.

"A spirit of fear" – now that's pretty easy to understand, right? It's when you live your life afraid of every little thing, always expecting the worst to happen and the other shoe to drop. It's when worry and anxiety become the rule rather than the exception. It basically means you're a scaredy-cat. So we appreciate the good news found in the latter half of this verse – that there is a remedy. We just have to have a spirit of "power, and of love, and of a sound mind."

That's where it gets a little murky for me. Just what does that kind of spirit look like and how does it operate, and how do I get it? Does it mean I should be able to simply make up my mind to be a stronger woman? Is that how the power part works? And if I have a spirit of love, does that presuppose I will never lose my temper again with people who irritate me or, for that matter, that I should never be irritated with them again in the first place? Do I need to read and study my fears away? Is that how I acquire a sound mind?

As I was thinking about all of this it occurred to me that the lynchpin to the whole verse is the word love. Here's my reasoning. If we could choose only one of the three antidotes to fear mentioned here, love would be the best option. Power and sanity are great attributes, but without the moderating effect of love they can be used in ways that do a lot of harm. Maybe we'd be less fearful, but we'd probably be less Christ-like as well.

One would think that the opposite of fear is something like peace or courage. But 1 John 4:18 tells us a surprising truth about that: the opposite of fear is *love*. Consider how each behaves. Love looks for ways to give; fear looks for the possible risks involved. Love thinks no evil; fear thinks of little else. Love believes all things, hopes all things; fear is highly suspicious. You be the judge: which of these is reflective of a powerful life and a healthy mind? Are you getting the picture?

If you want to fear less, love more. If you want more power and influence in your relationships, love more. If you want peace of mind, love more. "Perfect love casts out fear."

"There is no room in love for fear. Well-formed love banishes fear. Since fear is crippling, a fearful life — fear of death, fear of judgment — is one not yet fully formed in love."

I John 4:18

_____

_____

_____

_____

_____

_____

Day Twenty-Four

"I will bring praise, I will bring praise,
no weapon formed against me shall remain.
I will rejoice, I will declare
God is my victory and He is here.
All of my life, in every season,
You are still God, I have a reason to sing,
I have a reason to worship."

The Desert Song by Brooke Fraser

When we reflect on key moments in our lives we can usually picture exactly where we were, what time of day it was, who we were with, what we were doing, and perhaps even what we were wearing. There may even be certain sounds or smells we come to associate with that particular time and place for the rest of our days. Highly emotional events just have a way of sharpening our senses and perceptions and engraving themselves on our minds.

We all remember what it was like to hear about the terrorist attacks on 9/11 or, for those who are a little older, the assassination of a president, or man's first steps on the moon. Other events are more personal to us - the birth of a child, losing a job, receiving a frightening medical diagnosis, a daughter's wedding day. Occasions such as these find a permanent home in our minds and hearts.

Now, it may be because of my calling as a worship leader, but I have discovered that one of the most common things I recall in connection with my "life moments" will be a specific song. This is especially true of the darker, more difficult times I have walked through. Beautiful worship songs with lyrics that somehow ministered to my situation comprised a kind of "spiritual soundtrack" playing in the background through my seasons of trial. But there was more to it than that.

For there, always there – in the music – I have found the place where life comes back into focus and is doable again. There I have found the place where I can reconnect with my God. When I play, listen, sing, worship (whether in community or all by myself), and meditate on His Words – then comes clarity of mind and a renewed right spirit.

How do you connect with God, your Helper? Some of us do through music, some by reading the Bible or a good devotional, some by being out in nature, some by praying and listening. If you haven't found that place for yourself yet, seek it out. For in that place, days become brighter, fear diminishes, and hope and strength are tangible.

Father of Light and Hope,

Thank you for the refuge of worship and the restoration and comfort it brings. I give you my shame and fear. Help me to praise You, even amidst trouble, knowing my strength comes solely from You.

_____

_____

_____

_____

_____

_____

Day Twenty-Five

"Do not be afraid; you will not be put to shame. Do not fear disgrace; you will not be humiliated. You will forget the shame of your youth and remember no more the reproach of your widowhood."

Isaiah 54:4

I recall one wintry season in my life that lasted for several years. This journey was dark, lonely, and hidden, and comprised of daily steps that seemed to lead nowhere. The low point, I remember, was finding myself in the back of a dark closet, curled up in the corner, crying my eyes out.

I had been married for sixteen years. Through those years, circumstances had woven a terrible web of pain from which there seemed no possible way of escape. Being a preacher's kid who grew up following Christ, I did not want to even consider divorce. I relentlessly sought other solutions. But after years of counseling, praying, and laying fleeces out to God, He spoke very tangibly to me that I was going to have to do the very thing I did not want to do.

I had known a certain kind of fear in the years leading up to this difficult decision. It was a daily gnawing fear that grew at times when a change of surroundings was imminent. Now I found that the fear of those years paled in comparison to what it felt like stepping out on this unknown journey, wondering and worrying about what was going to happen to us, and what people might think or say about my failed marriage.

God was merciful to me as I faced this unfamiliar and difficult path. He brought me wise counselors and compassionate friends. He arranged downright miraculous circumstances of provision and protection for me and my children at times when we needed His help the most. And He supplied precious guidance through people knowledgeable in the Word and strong in their faith, people He knew I would listen to. These were ones who helped me to see that even this adverse turn of events could be God's will for my life, now that all other options had been exhausted.

As an additional measure of kindness and reassurance, the Lord led me to the scripture at the top of this page. Never had I read words more perfectly suited to a particular moment of need. I heard Him telling me in this verse that although what I was walking through was painful, scary, and something I did not want, He was bigger and His plan was greater than anything I would have to face. The fears that were gnawing at my heart would not come to pass, and I had nothing to be ashamed of. No fear; no shame. I clung only His promises to bring me through to the other side.

God wants great things for us. However, He will not always shelter us from hard journeys, especially those which are the result of our own actions. (After all, I chose that marriage relationship.) It is when we are forging new and difficult paths that God can do His most amazing work in us. If He is leading you on such a sojourn right now do not be afraid. Do not fear disgrace. Do not. Trust that you will hear from Him which way to go and what you should do. And you will, *if* you really listen – to His Word, to His counselors, to His own voice as you sit quietly before Him in prayer. Surround yourself with others who know Him well, and stay accountable to them. And do not listen to those who would shame you.

As one last morsel of encouragement, ponder this verse that an unknowing friend sent to me along that journey: *"God told them, 'I've never quit loving you and never will. Expect love, love, and more love! And so now I'll start over with you and build you up again. You'll resume your singing, grabbing tambourines and joining the dance.' "* (Jeremiah 31:4, The Message).

Dearest Sister, I hope you dance!

Dear God,

I commit to daily listening and learning from this verse. Give me the courage, Lord, to rebuild where I need to, and to join in Your dance! Amen!

_____

_____

_____

_____

_____

_____

Day Twenty-Six

"I have told you these things, so that in Me you may have peace. In this world you will have trouble. But take heart! I have overcome the world!"

John 16:32,33

Did you know that according to the bible of modern day psychiatry, the "Diagnostic and Statistical Manual of Mental Disorders", there are over 1,000 diagnosed fears that people seek treatment for? Can you believe that? And that's just the documented ones! Here's a partial list of the phobias and worries mental health professionals treat on a daily basis: mysophobia - fear of dirt and germs; mageirocophobia - fear of cooking (I think I might have this one); genuphobia - fear of knees (really?); ephebiphobia - fear of teenagers (this one I can thoroughly relate to); barophobia - fear of gravity; agliophobia - fear of pain; pteromerhanophobia - fear of flying; and last but not least, necrophobia - fear of death or dead things.

Fear is a very real emotion that can easily overtake sound decision-making and wreak havoc on our health and wellbeing. It can impact how we fill our time, where we go, what we think about, who we become on the inside and out. It is no exaggeration to say that fear can cripple and ruin lives. Is it any wonder, then, that the words, "Do not fear; don't be afraid," appear in one form or another at least 314 times in the Bible?

Jesus' words in John 16 are a paraphrase of that great directive. While it may be a normal reaction of the flesh to let fear and worry have their way in scary situations, Jesus gives us another alternative - one that flies in the face of human nature. He tells us He can give us peace. A peace that comes only through Him. Peace that we cannot drum up for ourselves. I believe the apostle Paul referred to it as the "peace that passes all understanding".

"...in *Me* you may have peace," Jesus says to us when fear sets its icy grip on our hearts. And why is that? "Because I have overcome the world," He answers. What fear did He not face as He carried out His life's mission to be our Savior? What opposition or enemy was able to overcome Him? Not even death, the chief among fears! Whatever victories He achieved, He achieved on our behalf and He shares them with us. His cross now stands between us and our fears and this is what Jesus reminds us of here. All we have to do is believe Him and accept what He holds out to us. That is how we have peace in the time of trouble through Christ.

God already knows we are going to struggle with fear and is not surprised or disappointed when we ask for help. The important thing is that we do just that and take Him up on His offer of God-given peace.

Alpha and Omega,

You are the beginning and the end, Lord. You know where I struggle with fear and just plain blow it. I want each day of this life You breathe into me to be lived with a full heart and an expectant spirit. I pray for courage and joy this day.

_____

_____

_____

_____

_____

_____

Day Twenty-Seven

"We know that God causes everything to work together for the good of those who love God and are called according to His purpose."

Romans 8:28

Some people really get confused by this verse. Does it mean that everything is going to work out the way I want it to? Will everything eventually have a happy ending if I pray hard enough? Will each situation work itself out if I just sit back and let it happen and keep the peace? Does working together for good mean that life will always be easy? No way. And yet, we are told this sublime truth: God works everything together for our good. Absolutely everything.

We eat a lot of crock-pot meals in our home. Looking at the hodge-podge of ingredients I throw in there before we all head off for work and school in the morning, it's hard to imagine that at the end of the day when I walk back in the door there'll be a fragrant, delicious meal waiting. That crock-pot takes all the spices and bitter herbs, the raw meats and hard vegetables, the broth and the seasonings, and after many hours of melding and heating them together, turns it all into something tender, flavorful, and nutritious to eat. How amazing! Isn't it even more amazing that God takes the bitter, hard, raw experiences of life and transforms them into things that feed and strengthen our spirit?

We see example after example of this in the Bible. David came through his season of sin to worship the God who chastens and forgives. Thus he became a man after God's own heart. Ruth, widowed and living on the edge, and faced with an uncertain future, chose to trust her mother-in-law's God in the moment of her desperation. God honored her by including her in the lineage of Christ Himself! Zaccheus was despised and hated for the unsavory character he was – tax collector and cheat. One meal with Jesus and he became forever heralded as a righteous and generous man. In God's Word we see person after person emerge from trials with new knowledge of the One who did the delivering. You know the feeling – when you know that you know there is a God in heaven and He is concerned about your life.

Battles with sin, affliction, or weakness can lead a person to the very place they need to be to meet the Savior. That is where God works His highest good out of what appears to us to be evil. From every painful or destructive situation, He forges a hunger of the soul that only He can satisfy, making us keenly aware of needs that only He can meet. He allows difficult things to come into our lives to serve a purpose far greater than what we can see. That's how we learn the simply difficult art of walking by faith and not by sight. All of it works together to drive us to Himself. And that's as good as it gets.

God of Wonder beyond my wildest dreams,

You are Holy, O Lord. You are mighty and just and the author of all good things. Thank You for melding the fragments of my life into something of beauty for Your glory. I stand amazed at Your craftsmanship. Lord, help me to let those things I know by faith penetrate and rule my heart.

_____

_____

_____

_____

_____

_____

Day Twenty-Eight

"For I know the plans I have for you, declares the Lord, plans to prosper you and not to harm you, plans to give you hope and a future. Then you will call on me and come and pray to me, and I will listen to you. You will seek me and find me when you seek me with all your heart."

Jeremiah 29:11-13

Rock on! That should be a verse we all keep on the dashboard! God's plans for each one of us are to prosper us and give us a hope and a future! Always!

I remember when I first memorized these words. It was at a Christian high school summer camp up in the mountains. This passage captivated me. It imprinted on my heart and mind in a powerful way. I had never heard such a far-reaching promise before. I didn't know this was how God felt about me. And I couldn't contain my excitement about the essence of what it said: God had a plan...for ME!

I was all in and could not wait to see what that plan was going to be! But as I moved further into adulthood, I started to realize that God's plan for my life was not matching up very well with my own. Things were happening that I most definitely had NOT planned on, and both my heart and my dreams got broken along the way. I couldn't understand why God wasn't keeping His great promise to me. I felt that He surely must have gotten the plan wrong. Or...perhaps I did.

I asked the Lord to show me what was wrong and He took me back to the words of Jeremiah 29 again. "Read it carefully," He said. I did that and this is what I learned. I had been all gung-ho to accept the promise part of that verse, but I had breezed over what was supposed to be my part of the deal. *"Seek Me with all your heart,"* He tells us, *then* all the rest of the good stuff in that verse comes into play. When I took an honest look, I knew I had not done as He had instructed. I had been so busy seeking what I thought would make me happy and secure, I neglected to look in the one place it could be found. And the course my life had taken as a result was far from the one He had wanted for me.

It took great work and faith to come back to my "great promise" and rest on it again. But I did. I have found that when I obey and follow through with the effort God requires (that is, to seek Him with all my heart and call on Him and pray to Him on a regular basis, everyday, as a way of life) God always shows me His heart and His gracious plans. Likewise, if you genuinely, fervently, desperately, and humbly call out to Him and seek His guidance – and practice this faithfully – He will do the same for you.

Trust me when I tell you, I want to follow His path. I want to know God so well that I clearly hear His voice. And, Dear Sister, that's what I want for you as well.

Your Word is amazing, O Lord.

I praise You and thank you for having a future and a hope planned for me!

_____

_____

_____

_____

_____

_____

Day Twenty-Nine

"Don't be bewildered or surprised when you go through the fiery trials ahead, for this is no strange, unusual thing that is going to happen to you."

I Peter 4:12

I lost my job. My teenager is rebelling. The diagnosis from the doctor is bad. There's something wrong with my baby. My retirement is gone. How can this be happening to me?

Why are we so surprised when life brings us such challenges? Why? When others are going through difficulties we seem to be able to maintain a hopeful outlook, but when trouble hits close to home, things look entirely different. We are frightened. We are worried. We have doubts.

And yet the Bible tells us many times that this life is not going to be easy. That is the cruel, raw truth. Nobody is immune to pain. And no one gets to go through life problem free. No one. Not even those perfect looking people that seem to have it all together. Life is a journey through trials - some big, some small, but they will surely come, one after another.

Any person that God has used in a mighty way has walked through adversity. Abraham was old, Jacob was insecure, Leah was ugly, Moses stuttered, David had an affair and committed murder, Naomi was a widow, Paul had poor health, Peter talked too much and it got him into trouble. But we are in even better company than that. Jesus Himself went through every trial imaginable.

In Hebrews 5:8 we are taught an astonishing thing: *"Though He was a Son, yet He learned obedience through what He suffered."* Surely we have a lot more to learn about obedience than Jesus ever did. And if our Heavenly Father's deepest desire for us is that we become like His Son, how, then, do we expect to live lives that are painless and problem-free? The apostle Peter knew better. He tells us that difficulties in life will not be the exception for the Christian, but rather the rule.

Here's the important thing to remember about the life experiences that assail us. It's not what happens to us, but what we do with what happens to us that counts. Maybe we aren't yet Christ-like enough to count it all joy, but we can trustingly acknowledge what God is up to when He allows hardships to come our way. Let us accept each trial as a gift God has given to refine us and mold us into the image of the One with whom we will spend eternity.

Father God,

Thank You for calling me Your child. Thank You Lord, that You will not forsake or leave me and You walk with me each day through whatever trial may creep in. I pray daily for eternal perspective that gives meaning and depth to each trial and celebration. May I be faithful in using each experience for Your glory!

_____

_____

_____

_____

_____

_____

Day Thirty

"Be strong and courageous. Do not be afraid or terrified because of them, for the Lord your God goes with you; He will never leave you nor forsake you."

Deuteronomy 31:6

What are you afraid of on a daily basis? We all encounter big life events that suddenly jump in and create a climate of uncertainty and doubt about our safety or wellbeing. Ill health, a car accident, or an earthquake can create fear like that in us. But I'm asking about those things that are rooted in the back of your mind and hold you back from fully living. Things that rob you of your peace and joy and the delight of loving and serving others. Or God. When you take that kind of inventory, what do you find? Is it that you might be "found out" and seen by others as you really are? Is there an anxious pang that the cancer might return? Are you afraid you might end up spending the rest of your life alone? If you are perfectionistic, you know the fear of failure. If you are shy, you know the fear of meeting new people. If you are insecure, you worry about how you will fit in. I'm sure you could add your own fear factors to my list. The point is, we are just as vulnerable to our inner fears as we are to external ones. Perhaps even more so. The question is, what can we do about that?

Well, the good news is that there *is* a remedy at hand. It consists of all the things the Word of God has to say about fear in our lives, and the situations that produce it. Consider these few examples of the plentiful fear-cancelling promises to be found in Scripture: Nothing can separate us from the love of God (Romans 8:35); God's perfect love casts fear out of us (1 John 4:18); Jesus died on the cross to destroy the works of the devil – and fear certainly ranks right up there as one of those (1 John 3:8); if we are afraid of loneliness, He promises to be with us (Deuteronomy 31:6, Hebrews 13:5); if we fear scarcity, He promises to supply all our needs (Philippians 4:10); if we fear the future, we have His promise for hope and redemption to come (Jeremiah 29:11); If we fear death, He promises to raise us up again to new life (John 6:40). No matter what fear the enemy could possibly come up with to throw at us, the Word of God has the antidote. It all boils down to knowing what the Lord has to say about the matter at hand and then choosing to believe that!

The God of the whole universe loves us to infinity and beyond and then some. His desire is for us to live rich, meaningful, nothing-held-back kind of lives. If we are hindered by fear, we've been lied to and are robbed of God's peace and purpose. There's no way I'm letting the enemy of my soul get away with that! I want to live with reckless, sold-out abandonment for Jesus Christ! I want to laugh 'til it hurts, cry 'til it's all dried up, serve 'til I'm completely spent, love 'til every drop is poured out, worship from here to eternity, and find more of God Himself in every day and every way. That's what fearless living looks like to me.

I hope I've enticed you to join me in trying this "strong and courageous" lifestyle on for size, jumping in with both feet and leaving fear behind. Armed with the knowledge of God's truth and the greatness of His love towards us, it can be ours. I want to slide into heaven's home plate someday, skidding in broadside, thoroughly used up, totally worn out, and loudly proclaiming, "Wow, what a ride!" Then I want to turn around and see you do it too.

Creator of All Things,

Thank You for Your perfect, unending love and care. I am so unworthy, but so grateful. Thank You for Your Word, where we find the truth of your plan, promises, and provision all laid out for us at the turn of every page. I long to live a life of joyful boldness loving You. I thank You for providing me the way to do so.

My prayer for you

Lord Jesus,

You are such an awesome God! Thank you for your grace, forgiveness, mercy, and strength that is new every day. Father, I lift up my sister today that has spent this last month seeking Your Word and wrestling with what it means to give you every part of her life. As she is striving to live a fearless life empowered by You and passionate about Your work in her life, I pray she would find You. And, I mean find You right in front of her with lights and bells on so she can't miss You answering her fleeces. Give her the strength she needs today Lord, to rest in You and run with You. May she be able to see past the challenging moments to the lifetime of character You desire for her. Bless her with joy — real, deep, genuine, God given, unwavering joy. May her willingness to hand over fears allow her to be used in significant, mighty ways for Your kingdom and glory.

And we give You all the praise and honor before, during and after each part of this journey.

In Jesus Name,

Amen